INTEGRITY RISKS AND RED FLAGS IN
WATER PROJECTS

JANUARY 2023

ASIAN DEVELOPMENT BANK

Corrigenda to ADB publications may be found at http://www.adb.org/publications/corrigenda.

Notes:
References in this publication to bidders, bids, bid evaluation committees, and bid evaluation
reports are used within the context of the procurement of works (contractors), goods (suppliers),
and consulting and non-consulting services.

All photos by ADB except when otherwise stated.

In this publication, "$" refers to United States dollars.

On the cover: **Water treatment facility in Georgia**. ADB's Urban Services Improvement
Investment Program will upgrade the water and sanitation facilities in Poti, Georgia
(photo by Eric Sales).

Cover design by Paolo Tan.

CONTENTS

TABLES, FIGURE, BOXES, AND CHECKLISTS

TABLES

FIGURE

BOXES

CHECKLISTS

FOREWORD

Since 2003, the Asian Development Bank's Office of Anticorruption and Integrity has conducted proactive integrity reviews (PIRs) to identify and address control weaknesses that give rise to integrity risks in ongoing sovereign operations. Insights from these PIRs are published in this series, *Integrity Risks and Red Flags*.

This publication highlights weaknesses and red flags identified through PIRs of 12 water projects financed by ADB. Further volumes in the series feature insights from five other sectors: agriculture, natural resources, and rural development; education; energy; health; and transport. Through this sector-based series, governments, public bodies, and stakeholders engaged in designing and implementing projects can learn from past vulnerabilities and establish processes and controls to effectively mitigate integrity risks.

To help foster and sustain economic growth, ADB's Strategy 2030 underscores the strengthening of governance and institutional capacity as an operational priority in the bank's developing member countries. Let us achieve a prosperous, inclusive, resilient, and sustainable Asia and the Pacific by maintaining the highest ethical standards.

John Versantvoort
Head, Office of Anticorruption and Integrity
Asian Development Bank

ACKNOWLEDGMENTS

Integrity Risks and Red Flags in Water Projects was prepared and developed collaboratively by H. Lorraine Wang (former advisor), Caridad Garrido Ortega (consultant and former senior integrity specialist), and Erickson Quijano (consultant) of the Preventive and Compliance Division, Office of Anticorruption and Integrity, Asian Development Bank.

This publication greatly benefited from the insights and comments of John Versantvoort (head), David Binns (former advisor), Lisa Kelaart-Courtney (director), Jung Min Han (senior integrity specialist), and Kristopher Marasigan (integrity officer) of the Office of Anticorruption and Integrity. This publication was made possible by reviews from Hanif Rahemtulla, principal public management specialist, and Alaysa Escandor, public management officer - Governance, Sustainable Development and Climate Change Department.

ABBREVIATIONS

AACT	average annual construction turnover
ADB	Asian Development Bank
BEC	bid evaluation committee
BER	bid evaluation report
OAI	Office of Anticorruption and Integrity
PIR	proactive integrity review

INTRODUCTION

Since the adoption of the Anticorruption Policy of the Asian Development Bank (ADB) in 1998, fighting corruption has become embedded in ADB's broader work in governance, public administration, and capacity development.[1] The Anticorruption Policy affirms the bank's zero tolerance for corruption and lays the groundwork for supporting anticorruption efforts.

ADB's Strategy 2030 identifies strengthening governance and institutional capacity as one of seven operational priorities for a prosperous, inclusive, resilient, and sustainable Asia and the Pacific. The Office of Anticorruption and Integrity (OAI) promotes the implementation of this operational priority through a combination of activities aimed at (i) enforcement and (ii) prevention and compliance.

The proactive integrity review (PIR) is a mechanism used by ADB since 2003 to help prevent and detect integrity violations and address risks in ADB-financed or -administered projects. PIRs (i) identify and assess integrity risks in procurement, contract and asset management, and financial management of a project; and (ii) recommend measures to mitigate these risks to ensure that project funds are used for their intended purposes.

PIRs evaluate the adherence of projects to three core principles of project integrity: (i) transparency—proper documentation of key decisions, public disclosure of project information, and protection of confidential information; (ii) fairness—objective and reliable bidding process and requirements optimizing competition, impartial evaluation, and a credible complaints mechanism; and (iii) accountability and control—accurate and timely project accounting and reporting, eligibility of expenditures and timely payments, adherence to contract provisions, and adequate project oversight and management.

OAI ensures that PIR knowledge is applied to the projects reviewed through follow-up reviews, at which time OAI verifies the implementation status of the PIR. In addition, OAI assists the executing and implementing agencies in addressing open recommendations.[2]

PIR knowledge is institutionalized in ADB operations through (i) embedding of PIR requirements in ADB guidance and instruction documents, (ii) integrity risk management reviews, (iii) knowledge enhancement and transfer workshops and other learning courses, and (iv) knowledge products.[3] Following a country-focused approach (one of three guiding principles outlined in Strategy 2030), PIR knowledge also informs the country partnership strategies of the developing member countries.[4] Through this exercise, PIR knowledge is considered in designing new projects as the country partnership strategy predominantly drives country operations business plans.

This publication presents integrity risks and red flags from PIRs of 12 water projects (Appendix) and highlights recommended measures to mitigate identified integrity risks.[5]

---

[1] ADB. 1998. *Anticorruption Policy*. Manila.

[2] The follow-up review reports document the implementation status of PIR recommendations (footnote 5).

[3] Through integrity risk management reviews, PIR knowledge is built in preapproval project documents (concept papers, reports and recommendations of the President to the Board of Directors, technical assistance reports).

[4] The country partnership strategy is the primary platform for defining ADB's operational focus in a developing member country.

[5] The water projects reviewed were selected from all active ADB-financed loan and grant projects using a risk-based selection process. The selection process took into account the size of funding, lending modality, implementation arrangements, number of awarded contracts, level of disbursements, input from relevant ADB departments, prior project results, external benchmarking, and potential benefits of a PIR to the project. PIR reports are available on the ADB website (*https://www.adb.org/who-we-are/integrity/proactive-integrity-review*).

SECTOR OVERVIEW

Like many of the world's precious resources, water is threatened by misuse, overuse, and pollution. In Asia and the Pacific, many countries are in a water crisis, and their expanding populations have increasing demands for water. "Water for All" is ADB's vision for the Asia and Pacific region. ADB works to increase investments for better water services in cities and rural communities and careful management of water resources.

Table 1: ADB's Financing Commitments in the Water Sector, 2017–2021

YEAR	2017	2018	2019	2020	2021
Value ($ million)	1,594	2,220	1,245	1,862	1,989
Percent of commitments in all sectors	7.32%	9.05%	5.18%	5.90%	8.74%

ADB = Asian Development Bank.
Source: ADB. 2022. ADB Annual Report 2021. Manila.

INTEGRITY RISKS AND RED FLAGS

Methodology

This report provides an overview of integrity-related vulnerabilities and red flags that OAI identified in its PIRs in the water sector.[6] A vulnerability is any gap in a project's implementation processes that, if not remediated in a timely manner, will increase the likelihood of an integrity violation occurring and/or the impact of an integrity violation. In other words, the vulnerability increases the integrity risk profile of the project.

Integrity risk is the risk that project funds are diverted from their intended purposes due to fraud, corruption, and other integrity violations.[7] Integrity violations are more likely to occur if integrity risks are not detected or not addressed effectively and in a timely manner. Integrity risk management is an essential prerequisite for ensuring that projects achieve the intended development outcomes.

OAI also assessed the level of vulnerabilities (high, medium, or low) by occurrence and impact.[8] This publication follows the project implementation processes and related subprocesses shown in Table 2. This document describes high- and medium-risk vulnerabilities and mitigating measures in each project implementation process.

Table 2: Project Implementation Processes

Process	Procurement	Contract and Asset Management	Financial Management
Subprocess	**A1 Bidding** Prequalification, bidding documents preparation, bid advertisements, submissions, and opening	**B1 Contract administration** The management of the day-to-day practicalities and administrative requirements under the contract	**C1 Expenditure management** Approval and processing of payments for project expenditures
	A2 Bid evaluation Assessment of bidders' compliance with bidding requirements, and preparation and approval of evaluation report	**B2 Output monitoring** Engagement with/supervision of contractors, consultants, and suppliers in relation to project outputs	**C2 Financial reporting** Project accounting and auditing
	A3 Contract award Post-bid evaluation activities until contract is awarded and signed	**B3 Asset control** Safeguarding and maintenance of project assets including asset inventory	

Note: The subprocesses reflect those prioritized by the Office of Anticorruption and Integrity and do not reflect all subprocesses that exist within each process.
Source: Office of Anticorruption and Integrity, Asian Development Bank.

---

6 Red flags are indicators of irregularities, which may indicate the occurrence of integrity violations. Project staff should be alert to red flags of integrity violations and promptly report potential violations to the OAI.

7 Integrity violation is any act which violates ADB's Anticorruption Policy, including corrupt, fraudulent, coercive, or collusive practice; abuse; conflict of interest; obstructive practice; violations of ADB sanctions; retaliation against whistleblowers and witnesses; and others, including failure to adhere to the highest ethical standards.

8 OAI determined the occurrence of a vulnerability by establishing the frequency with which this was identified in the PIRs; and based the impact of a vulnerability on the likelihood that this could have resulted in an integrity violation or misuse of project funds.

Integrity Risk Heat Maps

The heat map in Figure (a) shows the level of risk arising from the vulnerabilities identified in the PIRs of water projects and presented in the processes in which they manifested.[9] In the 12 water projects reviewed, OAI identified high integrity risks in all processes, i.e., procurement, contract and asset management, and financial management.

Figure (b) shows the risk level by subprocess. Risk levels are highest in bidding (A1), bid evaluation (A2), output monitoring (B2), and expenditure management (C1) subprocesses.

Figure: Integrity Risk Heat Maps

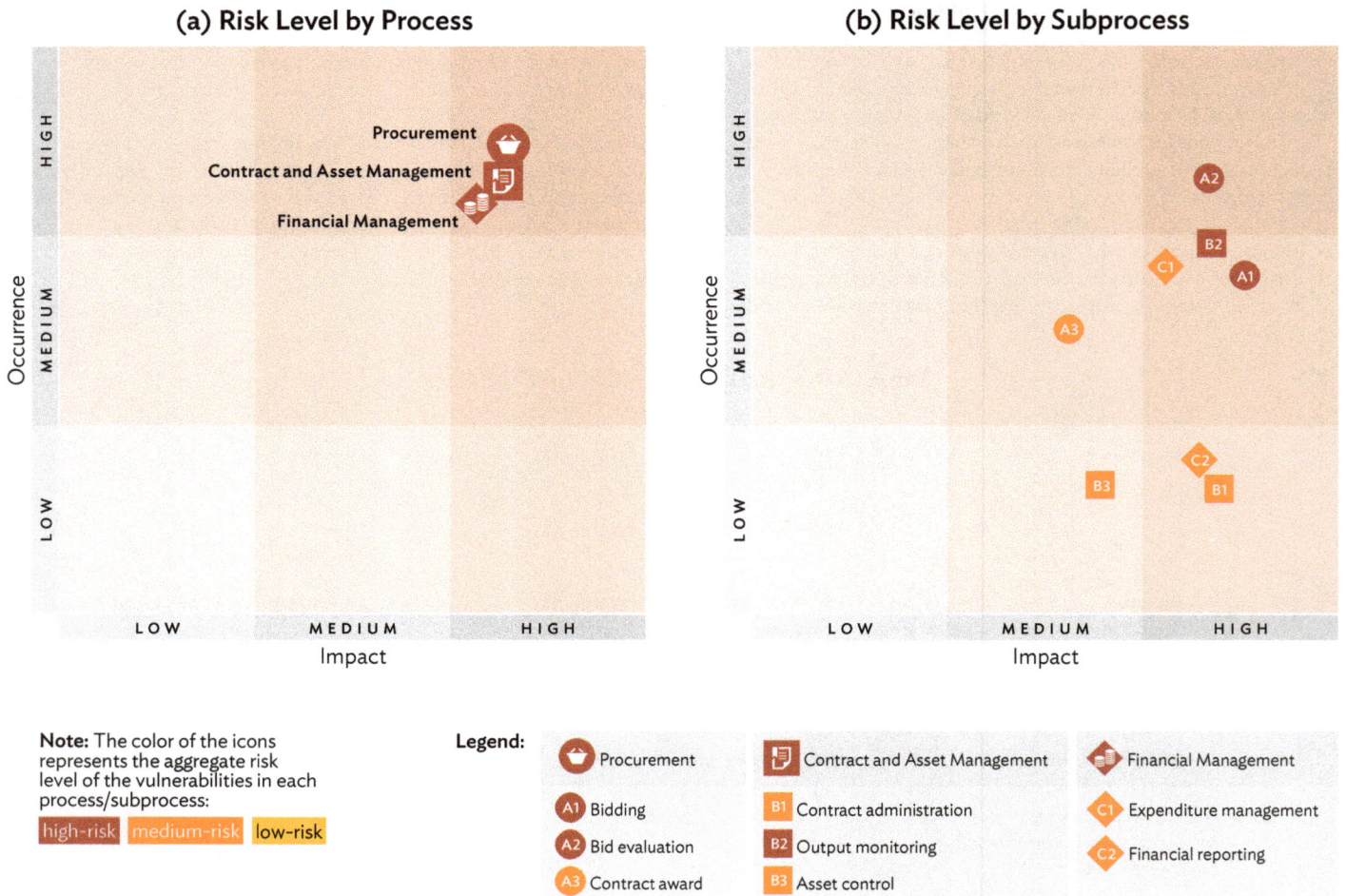

(a) Risk Level by Process

(b) Risk Level by Subprocess

Note: The color of the icons represents the aggregate risk level of the vulnerabilities in each process/subprocess: high-risk medium-risk low-risk

Legend:

- Procurement
- Contract and Asset Management
- Financial Management
- A1 Bidding
- A2 Bid evaluation
- A3 Contract award
- B1 Contract administration
- B2 Output monitoring
- B3 Asset control
- C1 Expenditure management
- C2 Financial reporting

Source: Office of Anticorruption and Integrity, Asian Development Bank.

---

9   The heat map is a visual representation of relationships among two sets of data: the likelihood that an integrity violation may occur (occurrence) and its potential impact to the project (impact).

Vulnerabilities and Mitigating Measures

OAI's analysis aimed to identify factors contributing to integrity vulnerabilities and to formulate risk mitigating measures. These measures may be applied to all projects regardless of their financing modality or structure. Project teams can use the due diligence checklists during bid evaluation (Checklist 1) and expenditure payment processing (Checklist 2) to identify and mitigate integrity risks.[10]

PROCUREMENT

(A1) Bidding

Red flags of integrity violations. OAI identified red flags that may have undermined the fairness of the bidding process. These increase the likelihood of fraud and corruption occurring, and thus may jeopardize the project and alienate prospective bidders. Examples of red flags in bidding are summarized in Table 3.

Red flags are multifaceted, and those summarized in Table 3 may have one or a combination of the elements of collusion, fraud, corruption, and/or conflicts of interest.

Table 3: Examples of Red Flags in Bidding

Type of Integrity Violation	Red Flags
Collusive practice	**Apparent connections between bidders** Bids under the same contract contained the same contact details and names of officers (also conflict of interest).
	Unusual bidding patterns, such as bid prices too close, too high, or too far apart It appeared that winning bidders were predetermined, and the contracts were awarded on a rotating basis. Bidders proposed similar items of the same brand and manufacturer. However, some bidders priced several line items unrealistically high—up to four times more than the engineer's cost estimates—possibly to increase the likelihood of the predetermined winning bidder being awarded the contract.
Fraudulent practice	**Inadequate supporting documentation** • The winning bidder proposed furniture that appeared to have been produced in a non-ADB member. The bidder omitted the manufacturer's nationality in its bid and possibly misled the bid evaluation committee. • Periods of employment with prior employers were not indicated in the individual résumés of the proposed staff, which raised concerns on the validity of work experience.
	Unreasonable statements Curricula vitae of five out of seven proposed personnel for seven different posts indicated the same 22 years of experience which was rather unusual.

continued on next page

---

[10] OAI rolled out project management checklists to help executing and implementing agencies to self-assess (i) executing/implementing agency capacity, (ii) project procurement processes, (iii) financial management, and (iv) project output management from an integrity perspective. These checklists are available at https://www.adb.org/who-we-are/integrity/proactive-integrity-review.

PROCUREMENT

CONTRACT
AND ASSET
MANAGEMENT

FINANCIAL
MANAGEMENT

OTHER
VULNERABILITIES

Table 3 *continued*

Type of Integrity Violation	Red Flags
Fraudulent practice	**Discrepancies between reported facts and observed data and supporting documentation** • The signatures affixed on a work certificate and post-contract award correspondence showed that the certificate may not be authentic. The certificate appeared to have been issued by the concerned bidder's representative, and not by the previous employer. • A bidder submitted a certification of ownership and lease of equipment that was issued by the lessor under the name of another bidder. However, the other bidder submitted a certification of ownership and lease for the same equipment from a different lessor.
Sanctions violation	The bid evaluation committee shortlisted a consulting firm debarred by ADB. The firm failed to notify the project management unit that ADB had declared the firm ineligible for ADB-financed projects.

ADB = Asian Development Bank.

Notes: 1. Collusive practice is an arrangement between two or more parties designed to achieve an improper purpose, including influencing improperly the actions of another party.
2. Fraudulent practice is any act or omission, including a misrepresentation, that knowingly or recklessly misleads, or attempts to mislead, a party to obtain a financial or other benefit or to avoid an obligation.
3. Conflict of interest is any situation in which a party has interests that could improperly influence a party's performance of official duties or responsibilities, contractual obligations, or compliance with applicable laws and regulations.

Source: Office of Anticorruption and Integrity, Asian Development Bank.

🔧 **MITIGATING MEASURES**
Red Flags of Integrity Violations

• ADB regional departments and resident missions should ensure that executing and/ or implementing agencies, including project implementing units and/or offices and evaluation committees, understand their obligations under ADB's Anticorruption Policy, including the obligation to report any integrity violation to OAI when such is initially identified or suspected. Executing and/or implementing agencies should communicate this to the bidders (contractors, consultants, suppliers); provide the necessary oversight; and conduct appropriate due diligence to minimize the risk of integrity violations on development projects.

• The executing agency should (i) establish procedures for all executing and implementing agency staff to disclose real or perceived conflict of interest with any bidders or other parties involved in the project and (ii) actively monitor its staff integrity and require them to adhere to the highest ethical standards.

(A2) Bid Evaluation

Vulnerabilities in bid evaluation can result in contracts awarded to unqualified bidders, thereby undermining the transparency and fairness of the procurement at an ultimate cost to the project. Process inconsistencies and deficiencies, and inaccurate evaluation results may create the impression of favoring a specific bidder. If not addressed, these vulnerabilities may eventually lead to substandard outputs, delayed implementation, waste, loss of funds, or harm to the intended beneficiaries.

Inadequate due diligence. Bidders may provide dubious information on their eligibility, financial capacity, and experience. Without adequate due diligence during bid evaluation, the bid evaluation committees (BECs) may fail to identify irregularities, inconsistencies, and/or potential misrepresentation.

Following a risk-based approach, the BEC should conduct due diligence to verify the submitted bid information against supporting documents (records check), from online sources (sanctions and other desktop research including previous adverse news), and/or from third parties (reference check). Combined with professional attributes such as a questioning mind and a critical assessment of documents, due diligence requires looking for indications of errors and/or misrepresentations on the documents, including checking the accuracy of information drawn from computations. The BEC should also seek clarifications/substantiation from bidders to the extent allowed by the bidding documents.

Examples of these evaluation errors resulting from the lack of, or inadequate due diligence are summarized in Table 4.

Table 4: Examples of Evaluation Errors

Bid Evaluation Aspect/ Requirement	Nature of Evaluation Error
Financial capacity	**Audited financial statements** • The bid evaluation committee (BEC) did not adequately assess the winning bidders' financial capacity as they submitted audited financial statements for only one financial accounting year instead of three recent historical years as required in the bidding documents. • The BEC did not validate the bidding forms against the supporting documents. Thus, the bid evaluation report did not reflect the inconsistencies between the figures in the bidding forms and the submitted audited financial statements. • The BEC considered the figures of the consolidated financial statements when the stand-alone audited financial statements of the bidder should have been used. • The BEC did not consider the impact of the modified or qualified audit opinions on the bidders' financial capacity, which could have significantly weakened the bidders' financial strength. • The BEC did not seek clarifications from bidders that submitted unaudited or incomplete financial statements. The bidding documents required submission of historical financial statements that were audited by a certified accountant, and are complete, including all notes to the financial statements. **Average annual construction turnover (AACT)** • The BEC used total revenue instead of construction revenue in computing the bidders' AACT. In some bids, the BEC did not use the available construction revenue information in the notes to the submitted financial statements to determine the appropriate revenue figures for its analysis. In other bids, the BEC did not confirm from bidders through bid clarifications the proportion of the total revenue amount that was derived from construction activities. • For one of the joint venture partners of the winning bidder, the auditor expressed qualified audit opinions on the construction revenue amounts for two financial years due to the questionable revenue accounting approach used. Nevertheless, the BEC used the turnover amounts from the audited financial statements for AACT calculation purposes. • Bidders used total turnover figures instead of construction turnover to derive annual construction turnover amounts that were, in effect, overstated. The BEC used the overstated turnover figures in its evaluation. ⚠️ 🅰️ • The AACT indicated a winning bid did not match the figures in its audited financial statements. The BEC accepted the AACT figures despite the discrepancies and even if these were not fully supported due to incomplete information in the notes to financial statements. Based on the audited revenues for prior years and historical revenue trend, the AACT requirements have not been met. ⚠️ 🅰️ **Credit lines** • The BEC accepted winning bidders' credit letters that were either due to expire before contract signing or did not indicate their validity period. • The remaining unutilized balances of the bidders' credit lines were not shown in the general credit line agreements or in a supplemental letter. Nevertheless, the BEC considered the maximum credit line amounts from all credit letters during bid evaluation without requesting information on unutilized credit line portions from either the concerned bidders or the issuing banks. • The BEC did not thoroughly scrutinize the validity of submitted credit facility or commitment funding letters. It did not seek clarifications from the bidder on the conditions of credit. The BEC also did not take into account letters containing redundant information, which may result in the same credit facility being considered twice in the evaluation.

continued on next page

PROCUREMENT

CONTRACT
AND ASSET
MANAGEMENT

FINANCIAL
MANAGEMENT

OTHER
VULNERABILITIES

Table 4 *continued*

Bid Evaluation Aspect/ Requirement	Nature of Evaluation Error
Financial capacity	**Current contract commitments** Winning bidders did not disclose ongoing contract commitments in their bids, which were identified from the review of the audited financial statements, specifically the bidders' asset size and AACT. The BEC did not seek clarifications from the bidders on this aspect, which could have given it more information that might have led to different evaluation outcomes. ⚠ A
Personnel	• Winning bidders did not submit the required documentation (e.g., curriculum vitae, related work experience certificate) for proper evaluation of proposed personnel's experience, yet the BEC assessed the bids as compliant with the manpower requirements. ⚠ B • The BEC evaluated some bids to have fully met the manpower requirements. However, the documents included in the bids (e.g., invalid course completion certificates and diploma for an irrelevant field of expertise) to substantiate compliance with manpower requirements were inadequate to support the evaluation conclusions. • The winning bidder proposed key personnel that would be deployed in two contracts that were funded by different ADB loans. These contracts had overlapping construction periods of 6 months to over a year, and the BEC did not check the conflict in availability of the personnel.
Experience	• The BEC relied on a bidder's self-certification of supplier experience rather than on third party-issued certifications (e.g., from previous buyers). The short period (2 days) between the date of self-certification received from the bidder and the bid evaluation report date strongly suggests that the BEC did not validate the bidder's experience. • A winning bidder accurately disclosed the amount of its participation (proportionate value of works performed) as subcontractor in a relevant contract. However, the BEC inappropriately considered the total contract price instead of the bidder's proportionate share in its evaluation of contracts of similar size and nature. • The BEC did not require the winning bidder to submit proof of compliance with the requirement for successful operation of proposed equipment subsequent to contract award (i.e., post-award condition). This cast doubt on the bidder's capacity to supply the required equipment. ⚠ B
Eligibility	• In respect of eligibility checking, the BEC reviewed only the nationality of the proposed subcontractors or suppliers and did not perform conflict of interest checks nor vetted bidders against ADB's Complete Sanctions List. • The date of the bidder's establishment as stated in its bid is 1 year before the establishment date recorded in the commercial register of its country's chamber of commerce. The BEC did not clarify this discrepancy with the bidder. ⚠ A
Bid validity	Bidders indicated bid validity periods that were between 10 to 46 days short of the required 60 days, yet the BEC accepted these bids.

Legend: ⚠ = indicative of potential integrity violation.

 A = Indicative of potential misrepresentation (fraudulent practice). Fraudulent practice is any act or omission, including a misrepresentation, that knowingly or recklessly misleads, or attempts to mislead, a party to obtain a financial or other benefit or to avoid an obligation.

 B = Indicative of potential bid manipulation (collusive practice). Collusive practice is an arrangement between two or more parties designed to achieve an improper purpose, including influencing improperly the actions of another party.

Source: Office of Anticorruption and Integrity, Asian Development Bank.

Inconsistent application of bid evaluation criteria. This may give the perception of favoritism or undue influence. Examples of inconsistent application of bid evaluation criteria are summarized in Table 5.

Table 5: Examples of Inconsistent Application of Bid Evaluation Criteria

Bid Evaluation Aspect/Requirement	Nature of Inconsistent Application of Bid Evaluation Criteria
Financial capacity	• In one contract, the bid evaluation committee (BEC) incorrectly disregarded the time deposits of a bidder, despite these qualifying as liquid assets. In another contract, the same BEC included time deposits in calculating liquid assets. • In one contract, the BEC considered only either credit facility letter or commitment funding letter to support a bidder's credit line. In another contract, the same BEC accepted both types of letters in calculating bidders' available financial resources. • In some cases, the BEC appropriately considered all current assets and credit lines as available sources of financing. In other cases, only either liquid assets or lines of credit were considered. ⚠

Legend: ⚠ = indicative of potential bid manipulation (collusive practice). Collusive practice is an arrangement between two or more parties designed to achieve an improper purpose, including influencing improperly the actions of another party.
Source: Office of Anticorruption and Integrity, Asian Development Bank.

Incorrect evaluation procedure and/or scoring. This may also give credence to perceptions of favoritism or improper influence. Examples of incorrect evaluation procedure and/or scoring are summarized in Table 6.

Table 6: Examples of Incorrect Evaluation Procedures and Scoring

Bid Evaluation Report Item	Nature of Incomplete Information in the Bid Evaluation Reports
Financial capacity	During evaluation of the availability of bidders' financial resources, the bid evaluation committee (BEC) incorrectly added the net noncurrent assets to the (i) working capital (net current assets) and (ii) credit lines of bidders.
Eligibility	One bidder was disqualified because it was in the "blacklist." However, the executing agency was unable to identify the source for the mentioned blacklist, disclose the party who imposed the sanction, nor justify why the bidder was declared ineligible. ⚠
Bill-of-quantity prices (BOQ)	The BEC filled in missing prices for selected BOQ items in a winning bid using quoted prices from another bid that the same bidder submitted for a different contract. ⚠

Legend: ⚠ = indicative of potential bid manipulation (collusive practice). Collusive practice is an arrangement between two or more parties designed to achieve an improper purpose, including influencing improperly the actions of another party.
Source: Office of Anticorruption and Integrity, Asian Development Bank.

PROCUREMENT

CONTRACT
AND ASSET
MANAGEMENT

FINANCIAL
MANAGEMENT

OTHER
VULNERABILITIES

MITIGATING MEASURES
Vulnerabilities in Bid Evaluation

- BEC members should undergo detailed and practical hands-on training on all aspects of bid evaluation, especially due diligence, before undertaking new bid evaluation assignments. Support from ADB regional departments, supervision consultants, and engaged procurement experts is required (a checklist on how to avoid common errors/lapses in bid evaluation is on Checklist 1).

- ADB regional departments should perform rigorous review of bid evaluation reports (BERs), particularly when the executing agency's procurement capacity is not robust or when contracts are high-value, high-risk, or complex. Rigorous review entails seeking clarifications from the executing and/or implementing agencies, calling in bids on a sample basis, validating evaluation report information against bids, and assessing the reasonableness of significant evaluation committee decisions.

- The executing and/or implementing agency should hold pre-bid meetings for high-value, high-risk, or complex procurements, where bidding requirements are carefully discussed with bidders. The BEC must consistently apply these requirements.

- The executing and/or implementing agency should check accuracy and completeness of information in BERs before submitting these for ADB's approval. For transparency, decisions made and justifications for deviations noted should be properly documented in the BERs.

Checklist 1: How to Avoid Common Errors and Lapses in Bid Evaluation

ADB Sanctions List

☐ Verify that the bidder (all parties to the joint venture/association/consortium agreement) is not on ADB's complete Sanctions List (https://sanctions.adb.org).

Construction Turnover

☐ Verify the turnover declared on the bidding form against the turnover reported in the audited financial statements submitted.

Financial Capacity

☐ Verify the financial capacity-related accounts (working capital, net worth) declared on the bidding form against the corresponding accounts in the audited financial statements submitted.

☐ Verify the credit lines declared against the supporting documents submitted.

Current Contract Commitments

☐ Verify the current contract commitments declared on the bidding form against the contract commitments reported in the audited financial statements submitted.

Experience

☐ Verify the experience declared in the bidding form against the work completion certificates (for works) and curricula vitae (for experts/consultants) submitted.

Pending Litigation

☐ Verify the pending litigations declared on the bidding form against the pending litigation disclosures in the audited financial statements submitted.

Criteria Requiring Computations

☐ Recompute the amounts on the bidding forms and verify that the formula used, including the exchange rates, are correct.

ADB = Asian Development Bank, OAI = Office of Anticorruption and Integrity.
Note: Where a red flag is identified, refer it to OAI for further verification.
Source: Office of Anticorruption and Integrity, Asian Development Bank.

(A3) Contract Award

Nonpublication of contract award. The transparency of the bidding process is diminished when contract award details are not published in a timely manner. This may lead to concerns on integrity of the bidding process and questions from bidders on the fairness of evaluation.

MITIGATING MEASURES
Nonpublication of Contract Award

The executing agency should publish the contract award notice immediately after receiving ADB's no-objection. ADB regional departments, in the no-objection letter, should highlight the requirement to immediately publish the award notice.

CONTRACT AND ASSET MANAGEMENT

B1 Contract Administration

Deficient guarantees and warranties. Without adequate and valid advance payment guarantees and warranty coverage, the executing agency would have no recourse if the supplier/contractor fails to fulfill its performance and warranty obligations. Examples of these deficiencies are in Table 7.

Table 7: Examples of Guarantee and Warranty Deficiencies

Item	Guarantee/Warranty Deficiency
Bank guarantee for advance payment	• The contractor did not provide an unconditional bank guarantee for the advance payment received. • The amounts of advances paid to the contractors were greater than the advances that should have been paid according to the contract. The contractors did not increase their bank guarantee to match the actual advances they received.
Warranties	• No warranties were provided for pipes delivered in the three sites inspected by the PIR engineer. • Civil works contracts had no warranty stipulations for the pipes.

PIR = proactive integrity review.
Source: Office of Anticorruption and Integrity, Asian Development Bank.

PROCUREMENT

CONTRACT
AND ASSET
MANAGEMENT

FINANCIAL
MANAGEMENT

OTHER
VULNERABILITIES

MITIGATING MEASURES
Guarantee and Warranty
Deficiencies

- The executing and/or implementing agencies should obtain adequate advance payment guarantees from contractors. In cases of delay in completion of services, the contractor should be requested to either extend the validity period or increase the amount of the bank guarantee.

- The executing and/or implementing agencies should include a warranty provision for project assets in contracts. This provision should be enforced on the suppliers and contractors to hold them accountable for any asset defects.

B2 Output Monitoring

Use of substandard materials and works that were substandard, defective, or off-specifications.
Executing and implementing agencies should ensure that contractors are adequately supervised and that any issues are addressed in a timely manner. The PIR asset inspection of water projects identified output defects, deviations from approved designs/specifications, and use of substandard materials, which could have been detected and rectified earlier had the project supervision been more robust. The inadequate supervision of contractors by supervision consultants and executing and/or implementing agencies resulted in delays, acceptance of works that were substandard, and cost overruns. Examples of related cases that the PIR team observed are in Table 8. Box 1 shows a case of a project vulnerable to unsuccessful delivery of output due to procurement and output monitoring vulnerabilities.

Table 8: Examples of Use of Substandard Materials and Works That Were Substandard, Defective, or Off-Specifications

Output Deficiency	Details
Defective road and bridge works	**The on-site inspection noted the following:** • Potholes on several stretches of road construction. • Erosion of selected stretches on the wet-mix macadam layer, where potholes were seen. • Porous abutment and heavy rust in steel truss on bridge works, as well as improperly built bridge span support.
Substandard materials	The contractor did not subject all installed pipes to pressure testing, i.e., only 8.5% of the total installed pipes were tested. The issued test reports did not identify which pipes were tested and compliant with the requirements.
Substandard and off-specifications water works	In six subprojects, leakages were found in installed pipes, connecting points of regulating valves, supply pits, reinforcement in the pits, and pump gaskets. In two subprojects, repainting and repairs were poorly done on the guard houses and drainage, as paint and grouts were peeling and falling off.

Source: Office of Anticorruption and Integrity, Asian Development Bank.

Box 1: Case—Irregularities in Civil Works Contracts of a Water Sector Project

Civil Works Contracts of a Water Sector Project Vulnerable to Unsuccessful Delivery of Output Due to Procurement and Output Monitoring Vulnerabilities

The proactive integrity review (PIR) disclosed red flags and deficiencies in the outputs of 10 subprojects inspected, which may have been a result of vulnerabilities in procurement or output monitoring procedures.

Procurement Vulnerabilities

Inadequate due diligence of bid submissions. In 45% of the contracts reviewed, the completeness of bids and eligibility of bidders were not examined before evaluating bidders' technical capacity. The bid validity of three bids for two subprojects were short of the required 60 days, yet those bids were accepted.

Incomplete and inaccurate bid evaluation reports. Many BERs did not fully disclose relevant bid information or contained inaccurate assessments. This irregularity posed a significant risk to the project as ADB's no-objection may have been given based on inaccurate BERs.

Questionable disqualification of losing bidders (red flag of bid manipulation). Several losing bids were unfairly disqualified, which suggest unfair competition and unequal opportunities for bidders. In a subproject, for example, there was

no clear basis for awarding the contract to the winning bidder as the bid evaluation committee (BEC) did not properly document its assessment of the available financial resources of a losing bidder's offering the lowest price.

Output Monitoring Vulnerabilities

The executing agency did not engage an independent technical supervision consultant as required by the project to ensure quality oversight by a third party. Instead, the executing agency performed the tasks of the technical supervision consultant. Lack of an external technical supervision consultant contributed to the inadequacy of design, substandard quality, and irregularities in the civil works subprojects, which increased the risk of payment for works that were incomplete and off-specifications.

TAKEAWAY

Procurement irregularities and weak project management and supervision had significantly impaired the project performance and quality of project outputs. If not mitigated, these weaknesses will impact the sustainability of this highly decentralized project in the long term.

ADB = Asian Development Bank.
Source: Office of Anticorruption and Integrity, Asian Development Bank.

MITIGATING MEASURES
Use of Substandard Materials and Works That Were Substandard, Defective, or Off-Specifications

- Erring contractors, consultants, and suppliers should be held accountable to ensure that they fulfill their contractual obligations. This entails enforcing relevant penalty clauses and reporting poor performance to ADB without delay.

- For decentralized, complex, or high-risk projects, independent third-party monitoring

firms should supplement the monitoring conducted by executing/implementing agencies and their supervision consultants.

- Executing/implementing agencies should closely monitor the supervision consultants. This entails rigorous review of the consultants' progress reports and, as necessary, verification of progress through field visits. A guide that provides a practical framework for field visits/asset inspections can be accessed through this link: https://www.adb.org/sites/default/files/institutional-document/431571/asset-inspection-project-integrity.pdf.

PROCUREMENT

**CONTRACT
AND ASSET
MANAGEMENT**

**FINANCIAL
MANAGEMENT**

OTHER
VULNERABILITIES

B3 Asset Control

Poor asset control and maintenance. If project assets are not adequately maintained, monitored, and protected from damage, deterioration, or loss, the benefits to the end users will be diminished, or worse, may cause harm to the beneficiaries. Examples of deficiencies in asset control and maintenance identified through asset inspections are summarized in Table 9.

Table 9: Examples of Deficiencies in Asset Control and Maintenance

Asset Maintenance Aspect	Deficiency
Defective road and bridge works	Project implementation units could not provide evidence of periodic inventory of project assets, which increased the risk of defective, stolen or lost assets remaining undetected.
Materials storage	Water distribution pipes and gravel were left uncovered in an open lot adjacent to the construction site, which increased the risk of accelerated wear and/or damage to construction materials due to exposure to the elements.
Works in progress	Excavated areas were not properly restored by relevant line departments, while construction was apparently suspended for a long time. This posed the risk of unintended delays in the project progress and contravention of the employer's requirements.

Source: Office of Anticorruption and Integrity, Asian Development Bank.

MITIGATING MEASURES
Poor Asset Control and Maintenance

- Erring contractors should be held accountable to ensure that they fulfill their contractual obligation to protect project assets during construction. This entails enforcing the defects rectification and relevant penalty clauses and reporting poor performance to ADB.

- Executing and/or implementing agencies should regularly monitor the project assets by periodic inventory and asset inspection to identify any misuse or abuse thereof.

FINANCIAL MANAGEMENT

C1 Expenditure Management

Ineligible expenditures. Executing and implementing agencies should counter the risk of payments made for ineligible expenditures. Expenditures that are (i) not within the contract terms, (ii) inadequately or inappropriately supported, or (iii) unauthorized expenditures are considered ineligible. These indicate that claims were not thoroughly reviewed against contract provisions. They provide opportunities for fraud and expose the project to the risk of loss of funds. Examples of these lapses in expenditure management are summarized in Table 10. Box 2 presents a sample case of ineligible expenditures.

Table 10: Examples of Ineligible Expenditures

Expenditure Category	Lapse/Gap in the Expenditure
Contractors' progress billings	• Advance payment for materials was made based only on photocopies of the invoices submitted by the contractor. • Claims were processed without the required, approved material test reports to validate compliance with quality standards specified in the contract. • Some details in the supporting documents in carbon copies were written in ink (i.e., not made in carbon copies) and used as supporting documentation. ⚠ • Line items (descriptions, quantities, dates, and/or values) in the billings were added, or otherwise changed. ⚠ • Some expenses were claimed and paid twice through separate invoices. ⚠ • Claims for one district were claimed and paid under another district. ⚠ • Supporting documents contained similar handwriting but from different suppliers. ⚠
Consultants' claims	• Consultancy firms submitted claims for reimbursable expenses (should be based on actual costs incurred) that were frequently in excess of what was expended. • The detailed cost breakdown of invoices submitted by individual consultants was not available. • The PIR team could not verify the existence of four individual consultants whose related expenses (including consultancy fees and reimbursable expenses) were claimed under a project. ⚠ • Claims for consultancy services were inconsistent with timesheets and/or other project documentation. ⚠ • Claimed amounts were in excess of contract terms. ⚠

PIR = proactive integrity review.

⚠ = indicative of potential misrepresentation or fraudulent practice. Fraudulent practice is any act or omission, including a misrepresentation, that knowingly or recklessly misleads, or attempts to mislead, a party to obtain a financial or other benefit or to avoid an obligation.

Source: Office of Anticorruption and Integrity, Asian Development Bank.

Box 2: Case—Ineligible Expenditures

Contractors' Progress Billings— Deficiencies in Material Test Reports

The executing agencies processed the following claims notwithstanding the deficiencies in material test reports (required supporting documents for payment):

• Material test results for some claims indicated compliance with specifications, but bitumen test for sand sample taken by proactive integrity review team revealed a lower density level of 1.13 kilogram per square centimeter (kg/cm^2) as compared to best practice standards of 2 kg/cm^2.

• Material test results submitted to support some claims were not signed by the design and supervision consultants.

• Some claims were not supported with material test reports to validate compliance with contract specifications.

TAKEAWAY

Claims supported by deficient material test reports should be withheld until the contractor replaces any substandard materials used or rectifies any defects in the project outputs resulting from the use of substandard materials.

Source: Office of Anticorruption and Integrity, Asian Development Bank.

PROCUREMENT

CONTRACT
AND ASSET
MANAGEMENT

FINANCIAL
MANAGEMENT

OTHER
VULNERABILITIES

⚒ MITIGATING MEASURES
Ineligible Expenditures

- Before endorsing claims for payment, executing and implementing agencies should ensure that (i) payment approval procedures are followed, (ii) supporting documents are checked for accuracy and completeness, and (iii) details in the claims are validated against the contracts and supporting documents. Payments should be refused or reduced in line with relevant contractual provisions for works or services that were not performed or goods that were not delivered (a checklist on how to avoid common errors/lapses in expenditure payment processing is provided on Checklist 2)

- ADB regional departments and resident missions should ensure that executing and implementing agencies, including project implementing units/offices, understand their obligations under ADB's Anticorruption Policy, especially the obligation to report any integrity violation to OAI without delay when such is initially identified or suspected.

Checklist 2: How to Avoid Common Errors and Lapses in Expenditure Payment Processing

All Types

☐ Verify the claim against the milestone payment terms stipulated in the contract (including contract variations).

☐ Check whether the payment information indicated in the claim matches with the payment information in the contract.

☐ Identify any red flags on the supporting documents submitted, e.g., erasures, alterations, or other errors and ask for clarifications.

Works (Contractors)

☐ Verify the claim against interim payment certificates/certificates of completion. Check if there are claims on non-workdays (work on a weekend or holiday with no preapproval).

Services (Consultants)

☐ Verify the remuneration claim (for input-based contracts) against detailed timesheets submitted.

☐ Verify claims for reimbursable expenses against supporting documents as required in the contract (not applicable for full lump-sum contracts), including:
  ○ Travel costs—proof of travel (tickets, receipts, boarding passes);
  ○ Accommodation—proof of stay (hotel bills, invoices, receipts); and
  ○ Seminars and workshops—attendance sheets, invoices or receipts for workshop costs like venue and equipment rental and refreshments.

Goods (Suppliers)

☐ Verify the claim against sales invoice and delivery receipt/proof that goods have been delivered, inspected, accepted, and, as necessary, properly installed.

Note: Where a red flag is identified, refer it to OAI for further verification.
Source: Office of Anticorruption and Integrity, Asian Development Bank.

⬦ Financial Reporting

Inadequate and unreliable accounting systems. To ensure that financial information is provided in a timely and accurate manner for project implementation and progress monitoring purposes, executing/implementing agencies should maintain adequate and reliable project accounting systems and apply accounting standards acceptable to ADB. Inadequate and unreliable systems increase (i) the risk of undetected integrity violations, noncompliance, and other irregularities; and (ii) the risk of making unsound project management decisions based on faulty financial information. Examples of accounting system and procedures deficiencies are summarized in Table 11.

Table 11: Examples of Accounting System Deficiencies

Accounting System Aspect	Deficiency
Financial records	• The project management unit failed to maintain contract ledgers. Consultant contract balances could only be determined by tracing transactions from the individual payment vouchers to determine accumulated payments and remaining balances for each consulting contract. • There was no records to track the United States-dollar equivalents of all related transactions, which hampered reconciliation of loan balances with ADB records. • Financial account descriptions were written in ink for descriptions, while values were written in pencil. ⚠ Ⓐ
Account reconciliations	Bank reconciliation statements were not in accordance with ADB requirements. Bank reconciliation statements reconciled only the withdrawal transactions per bank statement with disbursements per book. Furthermore, these were not reviewed to ensure accuracy.
Segregation of duties	An expert tasked to conduct internal audit of transactions had direct involvement in transactions processing, and prepared bank reconciliation statements and project financial reports. These incompatible duties exposed the expert to self-review.
Information flow	The project implementation units were not promptly providing the district agencies with pertinent project information. The district agencies were also the project beneficiaries that were ultimately responsible for sustaining the project output and maintaining project accounts. Information not shared with district agencies included works and services completion statements, acceptance and transfer reports, ADB loan and sub-loan amounts disbursed, interest accrued and paid, and/or project expenditures.

ADB = Asian Development Bank

Legend: ⚠ = indicative of potential integrity violation.

Ⓐ = Indicative of potential misrepresentation (fraudulent practice). Fraudulent practice is any act or omission, including a misrepresentation, that knowingly or recklessly misleads, or attempts to mislead, a party to obtain a financial or other benefit or to avoid an obligation.

Source: Office of Anticorruption and Integrity, Asian Development Bank.

PROCUREMENT

CONTRACT
AND ASSET
MANAGEMENT

FINANCIAL
MANAGEMENT

OTHER
VULNERABILITES

MITIGATING MEASURES
Inadequate and Unreliable
Accounting Systems

- The executing agency should (i) develop appropriate policies and procedures on maintaining adequate and reliable accounting systems, (ii) train all the project management agencies/units/offices on implementing the policies and procedures, and (iii) monitor their compliance with the policies and procedures.

The policies and procedures should include guidelines on maintaining financial records, performing account reconciliations, establishing segregation of duties, and accounting for project transactions. For this purpose, the executing agency is encouraged to implement a computerized accounting system, which would facilitate semi-automation of data entry and transactions review and generate real-time data.

OTHER VULNERABILITIES THAT CUT ACROSS PROJECT IMPLEMENTATION PROCESSES

Integrity risks in project implementation principally result from capacity gaps of the executing and implementing agencies—particularly in procurement, contract and asset management, financial management processes, and in maintaining project records.

D1 Executing and Implementing Agencies' Capacity

Inadequate technical capacity on ADB operational guidelines and procedures. Project staff of executing and implementing agencies should be knowledgeable on ADB procurement, financial management, and disbursement guidelines and procedures. Given the observed frequent staff turnover and high dependence on consultants, executing and implementing agencies should ensure that this institutional knowledge is retained, transferred, and refreshed.

MITIGATING MEASURES
Staff Capacity Issues

To ensure that institutional knowledge and practices over ADB operational guidelines and procedures are retained, transferred, and refreshed, executing and implementing agencies, with assistance from ADB as necessary, should develop an onboarding kit for new staff that includes primers and manuals. Regular relevant trainings should be undertaken for all staff and a quality assurance or monitoring process should be implemented under the guidance or assistance from ADB, as required.

CONCLUSION

Through its proactive integrity reviews of 12 water projects, ADB's Office of Anticorruption and Integrity identified vulnerabilities and red flags in (i) procurement, (ii) contract and asset management, and (iii) financial management processes. Key vulnerabilities are summarized in Table 12.

To manage related risks, ADB encourages project staff to apply the mitigating measures recommended in this publication and use the due diligence checklists for bid evaluation (Checklist 1) and expenditure payment processing (Checklist 2). Project staff must remain alert to red flags of integrity violations and report suspected violations to the Office of Anticorruption and Integrity.

Integrity risks are generally elevated in complex, decentralized projects (i.e., large-scale projects involving numerous project components, geographical locations, and implementing entities). These projects benefit from strong accountability and control mechanisms that clarify responsibilities at each implementation level (from the executing agency down to the last implementing unit), and from closer supervision by the executing agency and ADB. Integrity-related controls should be embedded in contracts, manuals, and other authoritative documents.

Under Operational Priority 7 of Strategy 2030, ADB has committed to support governments in their efforts to eradicate corruption and to implement anticorruption measures in all its projects and programs. We trust that the insights compiled in this publication will contribute to these endeavors.

Table 12: High- and Medium-Risk Vulnerabilities in Water Projects and Their Implications

Process	Subprocess	Vulnerability	Risk Implication
Procurement	**A1 Bidding**	Red flags of collusion (among bidders and executing agencies), fraudulent practice, and sanctions violation	Conflicts of interest, fraud and corruption, jeopardizing the project, and alienating prospective bidders
	A2 Bid evaluation	Inadequate due diligence, inconsistent application of bid evaluation criteria, and incorrect evaluation procedure and/or scoring	Diminished transparency and fairness of the bidding process resulting in contract awards to unqualified bidders
	A3 Contract award	Nonpublication of contract award	Diminished transparency of the bidding process resulting in bidders' complaints
Contract and asset management	**B1 Contract administration**	Deficient guarantees and warranties	Uncompensated losses caused by erring contractors or suppliers, and damages or losses on project assets
	B2 Output monitoring	Use of substandard materials and acceptance of works that were substandard, defective, or off-specifications resulting from the inadequate monitoring of contractors by executing/implementing agencies and supervision consultants	Implementation delays, inferior quality of outputs, and cost overruns
	B3 Asset control	Poor asset control and maintenance	Asset damage, deterioration, and losses resulting in reduced benefits to end users or harm to beneficiaries
Financial management	**C1 Expenditure management**	Ineligible, unsupported, or inaccurate expenditures being paid resulting from weaknesses in the review and analysis of claims	Heightened opportunities for fraud resulting in potential loss of project funds; potential threat to subsequent maintenance or warranty claims
	C2 Financial reporting	Inadequate and unreliable accounting systems	Greater risk of not detecting integrity violations, noncompliance, or other irregularities
			Flawed project management decisions based on inaccurate financial information

Source: Office of Anticorruption and Integrity, Asian Development Bank.

APPENDIX List of Proactive Integrity Reviews of Water Projects

Country	Project	PIR Report Issuance Date
Bhutan	Urban Infrastructure Development Project	Sep 2012
Georgia	Urban Services Improvement Investment Program – Tranches 3, 4, and 6 (follow-up)	Oct 2017 Jul 2019 *(follow-up)*
India	Multisector Project for Infrastructure Rehabilitation	Dec 2010
Indonesia	Community Water Services and Health Project	Feb 2011
Kyrgyz Republic	Community-Based Infrastructure Services Sector Project (Supplementary Grant)	Apr 2012
Sri Lanka	Greater Colombo Water and Wastewater Improvement Investment Project	Dec 2016 Sep 2018 *(follow-up)*
Uzbekistan	Urban Water Supply Project	Oct 2006
Viet Nam	Water Sector Investment Program – Tranches 1, 2, and 3	Oct 2019

PIR = proactive integrity review.

Note: Full PIR reports started to be published only in 2008. PIR reports prior to 2008 published on the Asian Development Bank (ADB) website only contain report abstracts/summaries. The Viet Nam Water Sector Investment Program has been counted as three separate projects: Tranche 1 (Sovereign Project 41456-023), Tranche 2 (Sovereign Project 41456-033), and Tranche 3 (Sovereign Project 41456-043). Similarly, the Georgia Urban Services Improvement Investment Program are three separate projects: Tranche 3 (Sovereign Project 43405-025), Tranche 4 (Sovereign Project 43405-026), and Tranche 6 (Sovereign Project 43405-028).

Source: Office of Anticorruption and Integrity, Asian Development Bank.